FOREWORD

2014 has proven to be a very volatile year in terms of world peace and development. The number of hot spots around our globe that effect the national security of the United States seems to have grown exponentially this year. These hot spots generally have a few things in common; one of which is the lack of a viable and defined transportation network. Generally they are hard to reach and have very long supply lines. There is an old maxim that an army fights on its stomach so you have to be able to move food to the front lines to feed it. It is also true that a country or region with a poor transportation system will generally starve and that creates unrest and dissent.

In this article LTC Allen and COL Albert identify how a strategic transportation vision and the discipline to build and maintain that network over several decades can start and enhance the growth of a country. Transportation is the backbone to a stable economy and it provides efficiencies that can help a struggling economy reverse its decline and prosper over the long term. The other points in the work also emphasize that a transportation system must be continually evaluated to ensure that it remains robust and maintained.

This piece is highly complex but once you understand the basic tenets I am sure you will find, as I did that if we do not pay close attention and continue developing a robust global transportation network, the world's economy and political climate will remain in a highly volatile condition.

Robert M. Carrothers
MG (ret), U.S. Army

ABSTRACT

Transportation is the "web of union", and sustainability of systems relies upon political will. Sustainable transportation is the result of intentional policy at the strategic level and potentiates unified governance and economic growth. This paper proposes that a long term vision and four key principles of sustainable transportation are critical to success in establishing and operating transportation systems. Sustainable transportation is integral to U.S security and prosperity, and a critical component in strategy for peace keeping and stability operations abroad. Sustainable transportation is both foundational to and interdependent with security and prosperity. Peace and stability are reliant upon sustainable transportation that can best be accomplished in a comprehensive approach starting with a long term vision and focused on balancing the key sustainability principles of transportation resilience, economic development, environmental health, and social values.

ABOUT THE AUTHOR

LIEUTENANT COLONEL JAMES P. ALLEN, Civilian: Safety and Design Technical Service Team, Federal Highway Administration Resource Center
Military: Deputy Commander, 206th Regional Support Group
Education: Masters in Strategic Studies, U.S. Army War College, Carlisle Barracks, PA, B.S. in Agricultural Engineering, Texas A&M University, College Station, TX, Registered Professional Engineer, Illinois.

Jim is a Safety and Design Engineer for the Resource Center Safety and Design Technical Services Team, Federal Highway Administration, U.S. Department of Transportation. In this position, Jim provides technology deployment and technical assistance in safety engineering and implementation of safety programs to state, local, and tribal partners. Jim is a registered Professional Engineer in the State of Illinois. He served as a Transportation Engineer from 2009-2013 at the FHWA Illinois Division with an assigned area of responsibility including 18 counties and 5 MPO's. Prior to joining FHWA, Jim gained valuable experience at the local, state, and federal levels of government through positions at the U.S. Army Corps of Engineers, Oklahoma State University as an Agricultural Safety and Health Engineer, a county highway department, and the Illinois DOT in Bridge Inspection and Highway Safety. He has over 20 years of professional experience ranging from planning, programming, design, construction, and operations of transportation systems, to university engineering and research, to military command responsibilities including civil works project oversight and construction worldwide. Jim is also a Lieutenant Colonel in the U.S. Army Reserves and the Deputy Commander of the 206th Regional Support Group in Springfield, IL.

He lives in Lincoln, IL with Natalie, his wife of 20 years, and his three teenage daughters, Lurena, Haley, and Madelyn.

COLONEL BLACE C. ALBERT Colonel Blace C. Albert was born in Charlottesville, Virginia. He graduated from the United States Military Academy with a Bachelor's Degree in Aerospace Engineering and was commissioned a Second Lieutenant in the Corps of Engineers in 1991.

COL Albert's military service includes tours at Fort Bragg, NC; Fort Campbell, KY; Schofield Barracks, HI; and Fort Polk, LA. He was the commander of the 4th Brigade, 10th Mountain Division Special Troops Battalion and currently commands the 130th Engineer Brigade in Hawaii.

COL Albert taught in the Department of Civil and Mechanical Engineering at the United States Military Academy, and he served as the senior advisor for infrastructure at the U.S. Army's Peacekeeping and Stability Operations Institute from 2013 to 2014.

COL Albert has Master's Degrees in Engineering Management from the University of Missouri, Rolla (now Missouri S&T), Mechanical Engineering from the Georgia Institute of Technology, and Strategic Studies from the U.S. Army War College. He is also a licensed Professional Engineer in the state of Virginia.

SUSTAINABLE TRANSPORTATION: STRATEGY FOR SECURITY, PROSPERITY, AND PEACE

Introduction

"Transportation is the web of union," is a famous quote delivered by President Lyndon B. Johnson and engraved in stone at the south end of New Jersey Avenue in Washington D.C. along the "Transportation Walk" exhibit.[1] The comments were delivered on April 1, 1967 as the U.S. Department of Transportation was formed and began to oversee how transportation affects safety, mobility, economic growth, trade, the environment and national security. Two decades later, the Brundtland Commission Report entitled Our Common Future, the landmark proponent of sustainability concepts, stated "In the final analysis, sustainable development must rest on political will."[2]

This paper combines these two basic principles, that transportation is the web of union, and sustainability of systems relies upon political will, to assert that sustainable transportation is the result of intentional policy at the strategic level and potentiates unified governance and economic growth. This paper also proposes that a long term vision and four key principles of sustainable transportation are critical to success in establishing and operating transportation systems. Sustainable transportation is integral to U.S security and prosperity, and a critical component in strategy for peace keeping and stability operations abroad. Sustainable transportation is both foundational to and interdependent with security and prosperity. Peace and stability are reliant upon sustainable transportation that can best be accomplished in a comprehensive approach that starts with a long term vision and is focused on balancing the key sustainability principles of transportation resilience, economic development, environmental health, and social values. This paper also explores each of these components of transportation sustainability to describe the characteristics, identify related planning factors, and suggest performance measures to use when developing transportation systems that are sustainable.

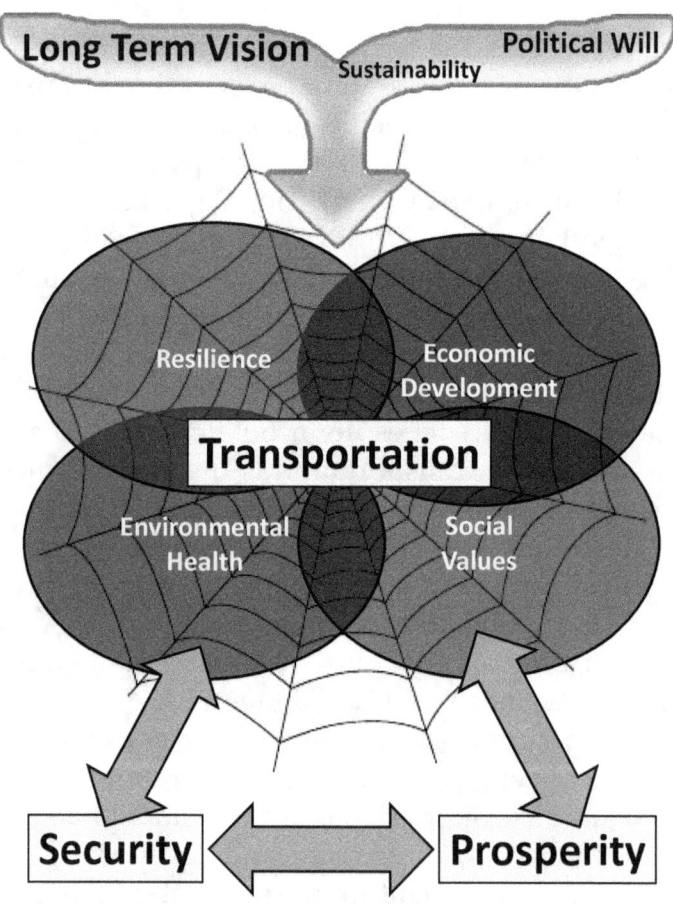

Transportation: A Foundation to Security and Prosperity, Past and Present

The links between transportation, security, and prosperity are demonstrated by the historical examples of past empires, the placement of transportation within rising China's development strategy, and the modern contribution of transportation in the U.S. rise to hegemonic power. Examination of successful synergistic relationships between these areas will educate policy makers and strategists in crafting future sustainable transportation development.

The ancient Romans demonstrated strategic use of transportation by construction of roads and ports as their borders and influence expanded. Roman militaries were generally charged with constructing roads and ports in new territories utilizing local materials.[3] The Roman road system extended from Britain to the Tigris-Euphrates Rivers and from the Danube River to Spain and northern Africa. The Romans built 50,000 miles of hard-surfaced highways, primarily for military reasons, but also realized great economic benefit.[4] Ports and roads served the dual purpose of a trade route that promoted prosperity and a mobility corridor that provided security. Transportation facilities that were planned to support military lines of communication became enablers of global power to deliver security, prosperity, and the *Pax Roma* (or Roman Peace) at the turn of the millennium.

The Han Dynasty and the Mongolian empire made significant use of transportation for both security and prosperity. The Silk Road was the most enduring trade route in history, being used for about 1,500 years, and reaching from Xian to Antioch and Constantinople.[5] As European powers developed maritime technologies from the 15th century forward, the Silk Road was eventually replaced by faster and cheaper shipping routes in the 16th century. Before leaving office as the U.S. Secretary of State, Hillary Clinton proposed a revival to the Silk Road as a comprehensive measure for creating peace and stability in adjacent countries. However, the lack of transportation resiliency in the inland region along the Silk Road has challenged contemporary efforts to regain prosperity and security in this corridor. China is learning from this and other historic lessons and making significant investment in multi-modal transportation infrastructure in a deterministic way.

China's transportation strategy is evident throughout its internal focus during the past several decades, and its more recent external focus as a regional hegemony. Huge investment in seaports, airports, roads, railways, and pipelines within China's borders in the last half of the 20th century bolstered national unity in a historically segregated and regionalized nation, while propelling wealth to a new middle and upper class and enhancing security responsiveness and defense within its borders. These internal transportation investments paid dramatic dividends in increased exports from China to make the United States their leading trading partner, even to the extreme that China and the United States have declared a current top priority to rebalance China trade from one less dependent on exports, to one jointly focused on internal consumer needs.[6] Chinese infrastructure investment in multi-modal transport systems will also provide the physical means for this shift in policy priority. China is engaging in a "Chinese Marshall Plan for Central Asia" through both political and financial elements.[7] The political element is an attempt to unite the region through development of transportation infrastructure.

The financial element includes development assistance to provide more efficient overland transportation and create a team of cooperative benefactors, rather than regional competitors.[8] China is using transportation policy and investment to create regional advantage in the global marketplace to broaden their national prosperity and security.

China views multi-modal transportation investment related to foreign policy through the lens of a Sun Tzu maxim, to win without fighting.[9] Understanding the current state of transportation in China informs the U.S. rebalance to Asia and the security challenges therein. As the Chinese People's Liberation Army (PLA) continues to modernize and expand its nuclear stockpile, China is now on the cusp of attaining a credible nuclear triad of land-based intercontinental ballistic missiles, submarine-launched ballistic missiles, and air dropped nuclear bombs. Chinese strategists view mobility in each modality as central to effectiveness and related to transportation resiliency. The dominant, land-based leg of China's triad also utilizes extensive subterranean storage and distribution infrastructure to ensure survivability against a strike or counterstrike.[10] With U.S. national strategy now elevating China and the Pacific region to a national security priority, predicting the strategic leverage and future direction of Chinese transportation in terms of security, economy, and sustainability is vital for the United States. It is equally important to examine the past and compare the current and future predicted state of transportation in the United States to inform strategic investment of limited resources for maximum benefit to national objectives.

As a nation founded by explorers and pilgrims, the United States evolved, and contemporarily applies, an innovative and strategic transportation policy that led to economic growth, stability, and global power. From the maritime based discovery of America as Western world powers attempted to expand their influence, to the formation of the U.S. Transportation Command (USTRANSCOM) by President Reagan as a functional combatant command under the Unified Command Plan, transportation was central to security, peace, and prosperity.[11]

Transportation that combined elements of public policy and private sector development, along with multiple modes, proved essential to U.S. prosperity and security. The first ferry-man, Edward Converse, charged one pence per person, or six pence per pig, for transportation between Boston and Charlestown across the Charles River in 1631, thereby providing a needed service and spurring economic development. In 1806, Thomas Jefferson signed a law authorizing the construction of the first federal highway, the National Road, citing that "better roads link the nation and allow people and goods to move inland".[12] The first transcontinental railroad was completed in the 1860's by a combination of government incentives and private investments and labor. Automobile ownership increased from 8,000 cars in 1900 when only 10 miles of concrete paved roads existed, to over eight million cars in 1920 when over 369,000 miles of public roads existed with hard surfaces. Orville Wright piloted the first powered flight in 1903, spurring the start of the age of aviation and eventually leading to the critical role of air power and aircraft carriers by the United States in the Allied victory of World War II. In 1956, the first containerized shipment that loaded full trailer bodies onto ships traveled from Newark, New Jersey to Houston, Texas and revolutionized the shipping industry with ripple effects into other transportation modes that still impact current multi-modal transload site design and operation.[13] Also in 1956, President Eisenhower signed a bill authorizing the National System of Interstate and Defense Highways to create a high-speed, limited access nationwide transportation network, along with the creation of the Highway Trust Fund as a public financing mechanism.[14] In 1987, the United States created USTRANSCOM with the mission to provide global air, sea, and land transportation to meet national security needs.[15] The evolution of transportation in the United States served the national vital interests and developed using all the components of sustainable transportation.

Components of Sustainable Transportation

Understanding sustainable transportation relies upon a common understanding of the concept. Accepted definitions vary slightly, but this paper uses commonly held views. Sustainable means meeting the needs of the present without compromising the ability of future generations to meet their own needs.[16] Transportation related to current U.S. policy is defined as the movement of people, goods, and services via sea, air, road, rail, or pipeline in a multi-modal system of systems. Thus, sustainable transportation is the movement of people, goods, and services in a multi-modal system and a manner that meets current and future needs. Sustainable transportation applied at the enterprise level starts with a long term vision and gives consideration to the four principles of transportation resilience, economic development, environmental health, and social values. These principles are connected and interdependent, similar to the interconnected nature of transportation, security, and prosperity already established in this paper.

The sustainability "triple bottom line" adopted by the United States Department of Transportation (US-DOT), Federal Highway Administration includes the three areas of economics, environment, and social values.[17] Transportation resilience, which encompasses the varied aspects of system and facility security and reliability, must be added to these as a key principle at the global and strategic level. USDOT applies the sustainable transportation concept by striking a balance in decisions among economic, environmental, and social values. Decisions must consider and balance transportation resilience as well in a global context and for peace keeping and stability operations. The goal of sustainable transportation then becomes the satisfaction of basic social and economic needs in the reliable movement of people and goods, both present and future, and the responsible use of natural resources, all while maintaining or improving the well-being of the environment on which life and the transportation system depends.[18]

Sustainable transportation applies across the whole transportation life cycle from system planning, to project development, to operations and maintenance. USDOT Federal Highway Administration developed a tool to support assessment and identification of sustainable transportation improvement opportunities. This tool is called the Infrastructure Voluntary Evaluation Sustainability Tool (INVEST), and may have interagency and intergovernmental utility to promote concepts in this paper in a whole of government approach. Transportation systems and projects serve many different and sometimes competing objectives including safety, security, mobility, economic development, environmental protection, livability, and asset management. A sustainable approach seeks to balance all of these needs while hitting economic targets for cost-effectiveness throughout a system or facilities life cycle.[19]

A description and analysis of each of the four key sustainable transportation principles (transportation resilience, economic development, environmental health, and social values) along with suggested planning factors and performance measures to be used by joint strategic and operational planners follows. However, a critical and initial element of sustainable transportation that provides unity of effort amongst sustainable principles is the establishment of a long term vision to guide government policy and private development and prioritize decisions.

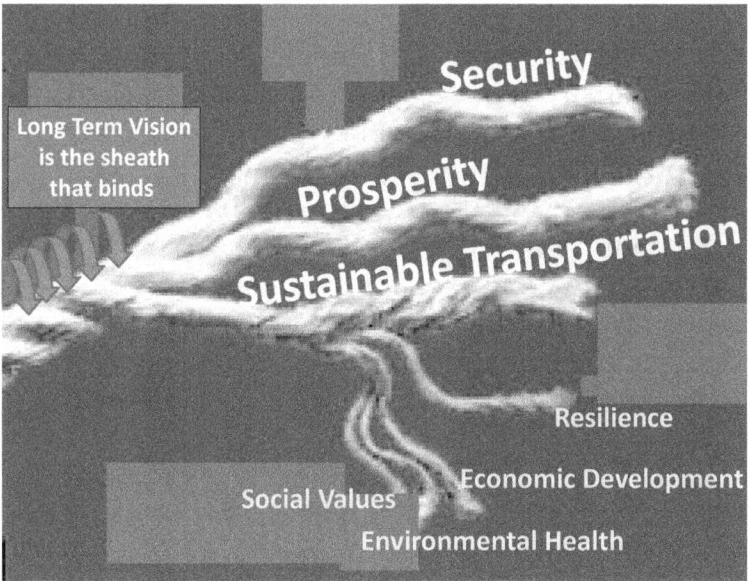

Visualize a wire rope cable composed of three primary strands (security, sustainable transportation, and prosperity) each interwoven, but each made up of individual wires as well.
The sheath around the outside of the wire ropes is a long term vision; and political will is the force pulling on the cable.

Long Term Vision

The successful historical examples of sustainable transportation cited previously in this paper shared a core characteristic of a long term vision. The Roman vision of an enduring and expanding empire drove the transportation developments in their governed regions. The Chinese vision of Asia-Pacific hegemony, free from undue foreign influence, is driving their current transportation boom. The Eisenhower vision for quick mobilization of military forces to theaters across either ocean inspired and guided the planning, design standards, and construction of the U.S. interstate system. A coherent and aptly communicated vision provided the unity of effort for these sustainable transportation endeavors. The requirement for a long term vision remains the first step in any effort to establish a sustainable transportation system today.

Sustainable transportation requires a long term vision to initiate and continually guide the process in a comprehensive approach. Lack of an overall vision or agreed "story line" is a recognized challenge and gap for stability and reconstruction efforts.[20] Conversely, a shared strategic vision allows different actors to work cooperatively toward the same goal. This vision is the "story line" that must be communicated by leadership, with mandates, and with the full participation of the host nation and transportation stakeholders.[21] Ownership of the vision may start with a few, but must become broad based for long term success. Crafting and selling this vision is ultimately the responsibility of the owners and operators of the transportation system itself. These often government, but sometimes private sector or nongovernment agency transportation stakeholders, should invest sufficient time in rational thought to plan and develop strategic goals and a long term vision that can leverage transportation to serve as a unifying effort with positive ends, capable ways, and sufficient means.

A sustainable transportation vision must focus on a sufficiently long time frame related to the envisioned strategic ends, while remaining flexible in the incremental and shorter term ways and means to achieve that vision. High level trade-offs between competing short and long term objectives are inherent for stabilization and reconstruction missions, however, the overarching long term vision must be kept prominent and govern the majority of decisions.[22] Lack of direction or vision at the enterprise or agency level is one of the highest risk factors that tend to result in unsustainable transportation endeavors. The timeframes generally used for the transportation planning process of 20 to 30 years is based upon investment planning which ties to economic development and financial sustainability; however, agencies need to consider incorporating longer-term social, climate and environmental change effects into their visioning scenarios and planning processes that also relate to transportation resilience and environmental health.[23] A long term vision adequate for the current and next generation is an ideal that adds the social value of considering impacts to children of the current and next generation while balancing sustainable components related to resiliency, economy, and the environment.

A long term vision which leads to an operational approach for sustainable transportation must account for the current maturity condition of the transportation system. Consideration of the current system ensures that the vision recognizes the real condition of transportation infrastructure, organizations, and processes that must be acted upon to move to the desired end state. Table 1 describes the American Association of State Highway and Transportation Officials (AASHTO) Transportation Asset Management Guide framework for five maturity level categories that are useful in assessing transportation systems and opportunities to move forward.

Table 1: Maturity Level Categories for Transportation Asset Management[24]

Maturity Level	General Description
Initial	No effective support from strategy, processes, or tools. There can be lack of motivation to improve.
Awakening	Recognition of a need and basic data collection. There is often reliance on heroic effort of individuals.
Structured	Shared understanding, motivation, and coordination. Development of processes and tools.
Proficient	Expectations and accountability drawn from strategy, asset management, processes, and tools.
Best Practice	Strategy, asset management, processes, and tools are routinely evaluated and improved.

These maturity levels are helpful in crafting a vision for sustainable transportation that moves elements of all four key principles forward on the scale. A long term vision establishes a strategy and prioritizes what critical transportation assets and linkages will be the focus moving forward. Key leaders within transportation agencies and interconnected fields must carry out the long term vision within their assigned areas by setting the direction, aligning the organization, developing a plan, and establishing tools, processes, and systems for implementation.[25] As a transportation system matures from one level to another, the long term vision will need revised. Strategic level planners can apply the suggested planning factors and performance measures in each of the four sustainable transportation areas to this scale to help inform the development of a long term vision, or set future objectives that help create a sustainable transportation system in line with the established long term vision.

Transportation Resilience

Resilience is defined as the capacity of a system to absorb disturbances and retain essential processes.[26] Transportation resilience can apply to either system or facility level and is the ability of the transportation infrastructure systems or facilities to anticipate and withstand disruptions, and recover rapidly from them.[27] A resilient transportation system is one that is robust enough to withstand severe blows, adaptive and responsive to threats, and can mitigate the consequences of threats through response and recovery operations.[28] Resiliency is not a single outcome, but rather a cradle-to-grave process for engineering, building, and operating a fault-tolerant, safe, secure, smart, efficient, and sustainable transportation infrastructure system.[29]

The United States currently considers transportation resilience as a critical component of sustainable transportation. The vision statement from the U.S. Infrastructure Protection Plan related to the transportation sector is "a secure and resilient transportation system, enabling legitimate travelers and goods to move without significant disruption of commerce, undue fear of harm, or loss of civil liberties."[30] This vision captures the close relationship between security and resilience, as well as the interdependent relationship to the economy and social values. Similar to veins in the body that make sure blood and oxygen are carried to cells, a network of transportation systems and multiple modes provides resilience by ensuring the transportation infrastructure is robust enough to withstand severe blows and provides adaptive responses and recovery operations.[31] Transportation system breadth and depth both provide attributes of resilience. Planning and designing infrastructure with current and future climate and threat impacts evaluated will provide transportation system resiliency.

Planning for transportation resilience in the face of potential hazards supports the other principles of sustainable transportation. Resilient systems operate under a long term vision and reduce long term spending on energy consumption and infrastructure replacement due to weather or climate change impacts and attacks. Resilient systems improve safety and security of multi-modal transportation system users and offer multiple options for delivery of people, goods, and services even when the system is strained. A well planned transportation system utilizes risk management to incorporate sustainable transportation principles.

Planning factors associated with transportation resilience help identify how resilient a specific system or facility is, and what risk response strategy is warranted or viable. There are four resilience elements proposed by the Volpe National Transportations System Center infrastructure resiliency framework: fault tolerance, adaptive solutions, critical asset redundancy, and mitigation.[32] Each element has associated management strategies and layered defense elements to improve resilience of the system.

Fault tolerant transportation systems and facilities have design-based components that ensure adequate functional capacity and structural hardiness. The system is built with protective measures enabling it to resist severe blows, absorb shocks, withstand extreme events with tolerable levels of loss, and degrade gracefully if needed.[33] An example of fault tolerance is the construction of bridges using seismic design criteria in earthquake prone regions or that withstand vessel impacts if they cross navigable water.

Adaptive solutions as part of a transportation system are capable of anticipating and preventing risks, limiting hazards, and ensuring continuity of operations through access to smart decision-making capabilities and situational awareness. Adaptive solutions enhance system resiliency by providing agility and flexibility for taking alternative paths and making real-time decisions to avert looming threats or mitigate developing dangers. An example of adaptive solutions is the National Oceanic and Atmospheric Administration's (NOAA) Search and Rescue Satellite Aided Tracking (SARSAT) system which serves as an automated adaptive decision-support tool that calculates precise location of mariners or vessels in distress, computes the probability of success for alternative approaches, and determines the most effective way to conduct search and rescue operations.[34]

Critical asset redundancy contributes to system resiliency by providing redundant system components and spare safeguards. Critical asset redundancy provides operational flexibility and distributed functionalities that would enable system operators and users to substitute assets and modes to avoid single-point failures. This flexibility enables the transportation system to reorganize rapidly, shift inputs and resources, and sustain an acceptable level of functionality as the disruption unfolds.[35] An example of critical asset redundancy is the presence of both rail mass transit and bus rapid transit for people movement in urban areas.

Mitigation as an element of transportation resilience is the ability to allay or ease the consequences of system failures through the system's response and recovery capabilities. Rapid response and recovery operations save lives, minimize the spread of hazards and their cascading effects, and reduce loss of valuable assets.[36] The NOAA SARSAT system combines adaptive solutions and mitigation strategies. Decentralized system operations and local government or private entities that are capable first responders to natural or manmade disasters are an example of mitigation that contributes to transportation resilience.

Risk response strategies depend upon the risk tolerance identified for a specific transportation system or facility. Risk response strategy options are along a continuum that can include: avoid the risk (remove the opportunity for a risk event to occur), transfer the risk (transfer the consequences to something or someone else), mitigate the risk (take actions to lessen the impact or likelihood of occurrence), or accept the risk (accept the potential impacts as tolerable).[37] Solutions can be incorporated into a long term plan by using a risk management approach that identifies current and future threats to the transportation system, assesses vulnerabilities and risk to the system, develops a strategy using risk-based prioritization, identifies opportunities for co-benefits and synergy across sectors, implements strategic options, and monitors and reevaluates implemented options.[38]

Many performance measures related to transportation resilience will apply to other areas of sustainable transportation. Transportation system condition may measure age, quantity, and quality of the system itself related to fault tolerance. Transportation security performance measures may include detection and elimination of threats, monitoring of unfolding events, search and rescue response time, or implementation of redundant paths. Public knowledge of the current and desired condition of the transportation system and resilient components may help receive 'buy-in' to infrastructure investments in line with the long term vision and serve the social value of open dialogue and a security-conscious populace. Safety performance measures should address both severity and frequency of safety issues and could include injuries and accidents of workers, crashes or injuries to system users or passengers, and claims. System reliability is simply measured by travel time from origin to destination or system delivery time, but can also integrate user expectations related to response time, comfort, convenience, and satisfaction within acceptable political frameworks for the region. System reliability measures are useful to establish political accountability and ensure consistency with social values and expectations in restoring normal operations after a damaging event.

A high level performance criteria proposed by the Volpe Center is "survivability" as a test of safety, security, and survival of the people, infrastructure assets, and the ecosystem; with a desired standard for the transportation system as "capable of withstanding damages with minimal adverse impacts – lost lives, ecological impacts, structural damage- on the people, transportation operations, economy, and the environment."[39] This criterion is useful in analyzing transportation resilience of a given system, but is also intertwined with the other three key principles of sustainable transportation.

Economic Development

Transportation infrastructure is viewed as both an input and output to a national economy. If transportation systems are developed in response to deliberate plans and cost-benefit analysis, they can dramatically increase the gross domestic product (GDP) of a given nation by enhancing private sector activities, lowering the cost of production, and opening new markets. Conversely, failure to provide appropriate transportation systems and services may hamper GDP growth by creating bottlenecks, increasing production and delivery costs, and preventing access to jobs and markets.[40] Sustainable transportation relies upon the key principle of economic development being incorporated into the plans, construction, and operation of the transportation system and facilities in a rational way consistent with the long term vision.

A sustainable economy is one in which people can pursue opportunities for livelihood within a predictable system of economic governance bound by law. Economic development principles will provide financial sustainability through the promotion of commerce and trade in cost effective ways. Strategists must address macroeconomic stabilization to finance transportation systems early on in the planning process as this is an often overlooked priority that may result in failure at the offset. Planners must consider revenue generation strategies to meet urgent demands of the transportation system as well as future improvements and expansion. These revenue generation strategies should stress simplicity to ensure efficient implementation during early stages of transportation system development, but may mature over time to become more complex.[41] Successful and financially enduring transportation systems combine public sector management with private sector competition.[42]

Economic development related to transportation sustainability involves internal elements related to the transportation system and facilities, and external elements related to system users and benefactors. Internal elements rely upon economic development that ensures short and long term financial viability in operating, maintaining, and expanding the system as it serves dynamic transportation needs. Internal planning factors include both public and private return on investment, integration of economic development with land use plans, and efficiency of system operations and maintenance. External elements rely upon economic development that provides movement of people, goods, and services, where and when they are needed, in a cost effective way. For post conflict scenarios, evidence shows that early attention to the fundamentals of economic growth increases the likelihood of preventing a return to conflict and encourages positive movement forward with renewed growth.[43]

A high level performance criteria proposed by the Volpe Center is efficiency, which requires that a transportation system perform its functions in order to meet its specified functional requirements (technical efficacy) at lowest cost (cost-effectiveness); with metrics including costs of building and maintaining a complex infrastructure system within the constraints of its technical performance, reliability, and service-continuity.[44] This proposed criterion precipitates multiple performance measures. System owners should establish and follow accepted budget and accounting standards for financial operations. Performance measures related to land use will ensure projects are consistent with long term and comprehensive plans that may include zoning, urban renewal, revitalization, or economic growth strategies at the national or local level. Metrics related to transportation demand models and transportation capacity can inform cost benefit analysis to ensure planners use reasonable assumptions on system use. Standardized and thorough cost estimating, which accounts for present and future worth, is a critical economic performance metric to compare estimated and actual system and facility costs.

Many performance measures related to economic development will apply to other areas of sustainable transportation. Affordability impacts economic development by encouraging system access in high density areas and in close proximity to existing or other planned transportation modes and nodes.[45] Affordability relates to environmental health indirectly as renewable resources or available materials must be incorporated into system construction to optimize costs. Affordability relates to social values by aspiring to serve all economic levels and cultural groups with access to jobs, health care, and government services, while still providing needed revenue to build, maintain, and operate the system. Metrics for life cycle cost entail energy use and overlap with environmental health to help minimize fuel consumption and associated air pollution and encourage recycled material uses. Performance measures that monitor timely maintenance activity and costs relate to transportation system resilience for system reliability, redundancy, and down time. Economic development measures will ensure longevity from a financial viewpoint, but sustainability of the transportation system will also depend upon environmental health.

Environmental Health

Examples of poor planning and minimal consideration of environmental health impacts in transportation abound. Shipping pollution and fisheries have damaged the ecology of sensitive coastal waters in Sri Lanka threatening endangered species and established cultural means of living.[46] Automotive emissions combined with coal burning and manufacturing produces smog that threatens individual human health on a regular basis in Beijing, China while limiting hopes of economic tourism.[47] The Trans-Amazonian Highway construction through the tropics in Brazil threatens deforestation of limited rain forest acreage and severs established ecosystems in the Amazon River basin.[48] A planned new airport on the south suburban side of Chicago may contribute to noise pollution and create extreme travel demand changes that result in drastic land use and cultural impacts as residences depart and commercial businesses swarm a given region.[49] These examples demonstrate why environmental health is a key principle of sustainable transportation, but also beg the question, "How should strategists and planners balance environmental health for sustainable transportation?"

Environmental health as a component of sustainable transportation relates to the current and future condition and quality of the physical and human environment. Transport has significant effects on the environment that requires planners and designers to explicitly address them in order to ensure sustainability is maintained with the natural environment. Environmental values and goals to consider may have global, regional, and local components for any specific transportation system or facility. Strategists and planners should consider environmental areas that include air quality, geology and soils, hydrology for ground and surface water, wildlife and habitat, and human health. Application of environmental health principles for sustainable transportation achieves goals in multiple areas including reducing life- and health-threatening environmental effects, making better use of readily available and cost-effective resources and technology, planning and managing land use and demand, and minimizing pollution and congestion through appropriate regulation.[50] These considerations and goals apply to all modes of transportation and can deliver a cumulative global environmental impact, but may vary in application based upon regional environments and policy objectives communicated in a long term vision.

The balance of modes in transportation should provide transportation resilience, while balancing both economic development and environmental health. Planners should document and analyze the environmental health impacts for possible transportation alternatives in concert with security and economic considerations within the context of the long term vision. Planning factors and strategies related to environmental health include public safety and health, biodiversity preservation, air quality management, watershed management, storm water management, energy plans, integrated natural resources management, and conservation plans.[51]

A high level performance criteria proposed by the Volpe Center is "sustainability" as an evaluation of the extent to which the system uses resources – natural, human, and manufactured – in a sustainable manner; with "sustainability" defined as a resource-use pattern that meets today's needs while protecting resources for future use. Metrics proposed include the extent to which transportation construction and operating inputs and resources are used in accordance with long-term economic and environmental standards developed for that specific system. To be sustainable related to environmental health, critical transportation infrastructure must be designed and operated within the context of their impacts on the surrounding ecosystems, including public health, now and in the future.[52]

Many performance measures related to environmental health will apply to other areas of sustainable transportation. Performance measures regarding air quality may include reduced emissions and ambient quality readings that reflect social values of the culture. Safety performance of the transportation system and safety initiatives aimed at reducing fatal and injury causing crashes or incidents apply to both public safety and health, as well as social values related to equity and quality of life. Measures for energy consumption can provide additional insights for fuel spending, greenhouse gas emissions, alternative energy sources, and energy independence related to economic growth and system resilience (if one energy resource is attacked or supply becomes limited by a natural disaster).[53] A comprehensive approach to reconstruction and stabilization promotes a balancing of all the sustainability principles by requiring nesting of short-term stabilization imperatives (quick need for resources and mobility) within the longer-term development objectives (enduring environmental health and transportation sustainability), and recommends a focus on the importance of a medium-term framework for distributing resources (measured aid to assist bridging short-term to long-term objectives).[54] This leads to the final transportation sustainability principle of social values.

Social Values

Social values as a key principle of sustainable transportation provides focus upon the human domain. The human dimension is the final arbiter of peace and war, thus the social value component of sustainable transportation cannot be overemphasized for enduring impacts and peace and stability operations. Maintaining the initiative with respect to sustaining the peace and setting conditions relies upon policies and strategies that give due consideration to the human domain.[55] Overt policy and planning considerations of social values ensures sustainable transportation does not overlook this critical area. Consideration of social values as a sustainability principle in transportation ensures that transportation investments reflect the unique vision, goals, and values of the community and culture which the system and facilities serve.[56]

To ensure cooperation consistent with regional social values, strategic planners and operators must understand cultural interests and organizations, and possess and demonstrate a high degree of sensitivity to those interests and operating cultures. Synergy is created when deliberate planning is conducted to provide cross cultural engagement in planning sustainable transportation. Regional engagement can tie all the components of sustainable transportation together (resilience, economic development, environmental health, and social values) through regional partnering that utilizes diplomacy, cooperation, and a shared vision.[57]

Social values weigh decidedly in post-conflict considerations. If inequity and discrimination were critical to a conflict, and they almost always are, they will be present in a new government's economic decision making, and often override considerations of economic efficiency.[58] Transportation systems promote civil-military objectives to support social well-being in post conflict scenarios that include access to and delivery of basic needs, right of displaced persons to return, healthcare, and supporting peaceful coexistence.[59] Engagement of disenfranchised stakeholders will require diplomacy and compromise, but can provide internal and external unity of effort if done well.

Many performance measures related to social values will apply to other areas of sustainable transportation. Accessibility to jobs ensures social equity and opportunity, but also relates directly to economic health. Safety measures demonstrate social value of human life, but relate to environmental health and human factors from the standpoint of both public health equity and occupational well-being. Performance measures that reflect incorporation of social values into sustainable transportation can observe the broad areas of system planning, project development, and operations. Measures of engagement with stakeholders during system planning regarding frequency and quality, and equitable treatment of minority and majority stakeholders related to consistency and fairness, reflect depth of social value incorporation into the process. Project development measures could consider transportation system accessibility to all people groups (regardless of race or social class), habitat restoration, human relocation and reimbursement treatment, and scenic or recreational quality of facilities. Operations measures with significant social aspects include equitable hiring and decentralization, system maintenance and regional conditions, system accessibility and reliability regardless of region.[60]

Efforts to develop a socially acceptable transportation system aligned with core regional values and a long term vision will complement the other key principles of transportation resilience, economic development, and environmental health in establishing a sustainable transportation system. Sustainable transportation is foundational to national security and prosperity. These key principles can be applied to both the United States and to U.S. efforts around the globe in a whole of government approach.

Domestic Implications and Options

Sustainable transportation is relevant to contemporary domestic policy and practice. Maintaining robust, efficient, well-linked systems for moving people and goods is a matter of vital national interest.[61] However, as asserted by the current Secretary of Transportation Anthony Foxx, the United States faces a massive infrastructure deficit which, if not addressed, can cripple the U.S. economy.[62] There is clearly a need for a comprehensive U.S. policy which lays out a long term vision and incorporates the key elements of sustainable transportation to include transportation resilience, economic development, environmental health, and social values.

The American Society of Civil Engineers (ASCE) generates an infrastructure report card every four years reflecting the condition and performance of the U.S. infrastructure. ASCE uses an advisory council of its members and assigns the grades according to the following eight criteria: capacity, condition, funding, future need, operation and maintenance, public safety, resilience, and innovation. These criteria are a measure of long term sustainability. The 2013 ASCE Infrastructure Report Card graded the following transportation areas: aviation = D, bridges=C+, inland waterways=D-, ports=C, rail=C+, roads=D, transit=D, energy including pipeline and electric grid distribution=D+.[63] The overall assessment of U.S. transportation infrastructure as mediocre to poor is alarming considering the vital role of transportation in the national interests. The poor condition of transportation infrastructure, combined with the current lack of a coherent long term sustainable transportation strategy with viable ends, ways, and means to achieve strategic objectives, threatens long term viability of the U.S. transportation system. An essentially unsustainable transportation system creates high risk for national interest that must be addressed by policy makers.

Momentum and opportunity for a lasting transportation legacy now exists as the current administration has highlighted infrastructure improvements as part of the agenda, and the current transportation authorization bill expires.[64] A long term vision that incorporates sustainable transportation principles should be strategically communicated by national leadership to garner broad based support. A multi-modal transportation approach that considers system resilience based upon critical functionality and enhanced security at key multi-modal transfer locations to promote strategic redundancy in systems is needed. A financially sustainable funding mechanism that provides stability to long term capital improvement and investment strategies at federal, state, and local levels will allow comprehensive and integrated plans to be developed on a national and regional basis that spurs economic development. Stronger linkages from the transportation system, to human health, to improved safety and strategic crisis response should be emphasized, along with environmental preservation. The approach must be consistent with social values that engage system stakeholders, but maintain equity in accessibility, liberty, and justice. A strategic communication message must coherently market this long term vision in a multi-modal approach that garners broad based support across regions and agencies to be successful.

Peacekeeping and Stability Implications

The transportation principles discussed thus far have direct applicability to operations overseas in pursuit of national security interests. Whether executed during peace and stability operations (PSO) or as an investment to assist developing countries move further away from the possibility of violent conflict, sustainable transportation will be a critical component to success. Security and prosperity are intricately linked in a symbiotic relationship with sustainable transportation. U.S. doctrine acknowledges the importance of transportation. One of the cross-cutting principles found in *Guiding Principles for Stabilization and Reconstruction* is regional engagement. This cannot occur without cooperation facilitated by mutually beneficial transportation systems. It also describes the importance of transportation to the successful implementation of rule of law (RoL), growth of the economy, relocation of refugees and internally displaced personnel, and the prevention of disruption to peace.

Within joint doctrine, transportation is a part of the economic stabilization and infrastructure function. It is a means of implementing civil-military operation (CMO) tasks, it facilitates the disarmament, demobilization, and reintegration (DDR) process, and ensures the distribution of relief supplies during humanitarian assistance (HA) operations. NATO doctrine also mentions the importance of transportation to the electoral process during a political transition by moving ballot boxes and staff.[65]

There are examples throughout history that link the success of operations to the efforts placed on creating a sustainable transportation network. The British emphasized construction of airfields and roads in Malaya between 1947 and 1960. This resulted in improved security, a growing economy, and the eventual defeat of communist insurgents that were separated from the population. As transportation infrastructure was improved, engineers built to the standard of 'just good enough' to achieve the purpose, and projects always supported counterinsurgency objectives. On the other hand, in Vietnam where the U.S. effort was generally considered unsuccessful, the United States failed to include economic or political objectives while constructing infrastructure. Engineers were concerned primarily with force protection. "U.S. construction efforts remained steadfastly focused on the security line of operation with seemingly little attention paid to assisting the host nation in eradicating causes underlying insurgent motives."[66]

Recent examples demonstrating the importance of a resilient transportation network are just as common. A World Bank report argues the importance of transportation systems to link isolated communities. In developing countries, like many African nations that the report discusses, these transportation systems can be vital for access to water and sanitation much less as a means to improving economic well-being. A lack of transportation networks is extremely problematic during humanitarian assistance operations as those in Somalia demonstrated. The importance of transportation increases when conducting peace operations. Moving away from violent conflict in South Sudan has been problematic, because the lack of roads hampers security, sustainable macroeconomics, and the ability of the government to extend and maintain authority across the country. The importance of transportation is recognized in Afghanistan where road construction was the only infrastructure improvement that Afghans believed to improve stability. Many argue that creating the 'new silk road' in Afghanistan is the key to success there.[67] In recent remarks at the United Nations (U.N.), the U.S. Mission stated, "expanding connections to its Central Asian neighbors will greatly enhance Afghanistan's ability to diversify its economy, increase trade, and create more and better opportunities for its people."[68] In another detailed proposal, 10 of 22 infrastructure recommendations deal directly with transportation, and all of the others are supported by transportation. Additionally, the nodes facilitating the transfer of goods from one means of transportation to another are crucial to security and economic success. Iraq and its allies invested heavily in the railroad, aviation, and coastal port nodes, which greatly helped achieve the necessary stability objectives.[69]

Long Term Vision

As with domestic planning, transportation networks will not be sustainable in PSO, HA operations, or in assistance to developing countries without ensuring there is a long term vision. A domestic example occurred during Hurricane Katrina where evacuation routes were open and in good condition for use, but planners neglected to account for local population reliance upon public transportation. Today, countries bordering Afghanistan utilize three different rail gauges. Without a vision toward efficient transportation of mineral resources out of the country, through ports, and across a single type of rail gauge, Afghanistan will lose billions of dollars in unrealized revenue. Another example of vision (or lack thereof) is accounting for rapid urbanization following a conflict. Better opportunities generally exist in cities during this time. Population increased immensely in the capitols of Cambodia and Timor-Leste as conflicts ended. The same thing is now occurring in Kabul, and yet much of the transportation focus in Afghanistan was on projects like the Ring Road vice preparing for the urbanization of Afghanistan. A good example of long term transportation vision, coupled with sustainable economic development, is occurring in Timor-Leste where money from their petroleum-fed sovereign wealth fund is reinvested in transportation.[70] This policy continues to contribute to Timor-Leste's ability to move further and further from violent conflict.

Transportation Resilience

Assessing, repairing, designing, and building transportation systems utilizing the components of sustainable transportation-resilience, economic development, environmental health, and social value-is of vital importance. These components must be applied overseas during PSO, HA operations, and in developing nations just as they are domestically.

Transportation resilience describes a system that is robust, redundant, adaptive, and able to mitigate consequences. Most importantly during PSOs, however, transportation must be secure. The *Guiding Principles* describes one of the necessary endstates for stability as a Safe and Secure Environment. Within this context, securing transportation is essential to enabling humanitarian assistance and economic recovery.[71] The U.S. diplomacy and development community acknowledges that securing the physical safety of its citizens should be the top priority of any government, and without security, essential services such as transportation and others will not be delivered.[72] Even a casual study of stability operations concludes that transportation facilitates security and security enables transportation. What is less obvious, however, is the equally important focus on reducing barriers to transportation when providing transportation security. For example, a road might be secure from physical attacks thanks to police checkpoints located every mile along the route, but if each checkpoint is taking a bribe, the road will not be used and therefore not serve its enabling purposes. When this corruption exists at critical nodes, the barriers to transportation, and thereby social and economic improvement, are magnified. Additionally, in order to achieve stability objectives, transportation security should be linked to the campaign's information operations. A great example of this occurred in Sarajevo where citizens felt a return to normalcy as the streetcar system was brought back online. This transportation network was part of the culture and reflected the social values in this area, and therefore became a symbol of peace returning to their lives.[73]

Building this resiliency begins with an acute appreciation of the routes upon which goods and cash move between markets and homes. This is particularly important in the conduct of HA operations, because they normally follow a catastrophic event. Destruction of the transportation systems contribute to hunger and disease in these situations. No amount of prepositioning materials will overcome the requirement to move supplies via transportation routes following a humanitarian crisis. The resilience of a nation's transportation system during HA operations contributes directly to the overall resilience of a nation during crisis.[74] Another unique consideration during PSOs is whether secondary objectives (which may be the primary desired effect), such as increasing the influence of the government, are being accomplished. One report from Afghanistan indicated that the degrading roads that had initially been improved under the auspices of ISAF or the government served to separate the population from ISAF. Therefore, building transportation networks that are 'just good enough' but allow locals to sustain them is important to the resilience of the network.[75]

Economic Development

As stated earlier, sustainable transportation works symbiotically with security and prosperity. Without transportation, economic development can't occur and prosperity will be extremely isolated at best. According to the *Guiding Principles*, a sustainable economy is one of the five endstates for stabilization and reconstruction. This is achieved by meeting the following conditions: macroeconomic stabilization, control over the illicit economy and economic-based threats to peace, market economy sustainability, and employment generation.[76] USAID states that "early attention to the fundamentals of economic growth increases the likelihood of successfully preventing a return to conflict…is critically important to heed this evidence and make early economic interventions an integral part of a comprehensive restructuring and stabilization program."[77] USAID also describes infrastructure, including transportation, as "the productive backbone of any economy," and makes the point that high costs can greatly limit the ability of a nation to establish viable exports.[78] The Department of State's (DoS's) viewpoint is summed up in the title of an article, *Better Infrastructure Brings Economic Growth*, and states that building transportation networks not only creates jobs but increases societal wealth and standard of living. It is transportation that enables accomplishment of the four DoS pillars that comprise the U.S. strategy for economic growth in Afghanistan. The World Bank advocates for improving economic development through transportation in multiple documents. They point out that barriers to migration, such as transportation costs, must be reduced or eliminated in order for people to go where the jobs are, and states that roads are among the top five most important National Priority Programs for ensuring economic growth in Afghanistan. Transportation ensures products get to market, facilitates delivery of essential services, makes agriculture a viable means of employment, and allows a nation to capitalize on its natural resources.[79]

Environmental Health

At first blush, one might wonder just how much environmental health translates from domestic application to PSOs. The answer is that environmental health is universal in translation due to the human and long term impacts. Militaries argue that security and mission accomplishment trump the need to protect the environment. The problem with this argument is that it is a false dichotomy. The large majority of situations have a range of options that are more complex than a simple 'accomplish the mission or protect the environment,' particularly in PSOs where units are trying to achieve effects across a myriad of interconnected stability sectors. When operations do create damage, the faster and more robust the response to repair the environment, the cheaper and more effective it will be. The United Nations Environment Programme (UNEP) demonstrated this in Serbia and Montenegro. Targeted and rapid cleanup saved money and paid dividends throughout multiple stability sectors. UNEP's experience in these countries, and others like Afghanistan, Iraq, Liberia, Macedonia, Albania, Lebanon, Sudan, and the Palestinian territories, supports the assertion that environmental assistance be part of the post-disaster reconstruction agenda.[80]

History is replete with examples of nations not considering environmental health. Estonia housed about 570 Soviet bases at one time. In the mid-90s, the environmental cleanup associated with these bases was four times the country's budget. International law, though it has attempted to limit environmental consequences, does not have an effective means of enforcing accountability, and it does make provisions for military expediency. Cases where nations have contributed to repairing the environment come in two forms. The first is "victor's justice" such as Iraq paying for damages to Kuwait. This would not have occurred if the victors of Desert Storm had not imposed this upon Iraq. The second is when a nation deems it to be in their strategic interests to do so. Japan is currently assisting China with toxic waste they buried there during World War II. In 2008, the United States began to help clean up around Da Nang in Vietnam. In both cases, Japan and the United States were unwilling or uninterested in helping until the geopolitical impact was to their advantage. The United States believed it was important to assist Canada and Panama with cleaning up U.S. bases, but not the base at Subic Bay in the Philippines. The absolute best way to prevent a double standard that could damage bilateral relationships in the future, and to save the most money in the long run, is to plan for environmental health measures up front and ensure that they remain a relevant consideration throughout the execution of PSOs.[81]

If one doubts the importance of considering the environment while developing transportation infrastructure, they need but look at how natural resources such as diamonds in Angola or timber in Cambodia contributed to violent conflict and served as drivers of instability across multiple stability sectors. UNEP emphatically states that, "Environmental security, both for reducing the threat of war, and in successfully rehabilitating a country following conflict, must no long be viewed as a luxury but needs to be seen as a fundamental part of a long lasting peace policy."[82] The United States Army began to increase the emphasis placed on environmental considerations in 2009 when they created the Green Warrior Initiative. The first director, Colonel Tim Hill, stated that "counterinsurgency strategies should incorporate environmental considerations into everything they do." His role "is to 'change the culture of the Army,' to find ways to fight a counterinsurgency that considers environmental and sustainability issues."[83] The United States, fellow

Security Council members, and major troop contributing countries of the U.N. must continue this effort to elevate the importance of environmental health. When developing transportation infrastructure and systems, environmental health considerations will result in long term savings and improve the relationship with the host nation, thus increasing the probability of success across all stability sectors.

Social Values

The applicability of improving social values through transportation is very evident during PSOs. The stability framework contained in the interagency *Guiding Principles* manual includes Social Well-Being as one of the five necessary endstates. Of the four conditions required to achieve this endstate, there will be no chance of achieving three of them without a sustainable transportation network. First, the population must have access to and delivery of basic needs services. These services refer to the minimum standards for water, food, shelter, and health as described by The Sphere Project and adopted internationally.[84] Second, the population must have access to and delivery of education. This must be equal access to all sectors of the population. Third, there is a right of return and resettlement for refugees and internally displaced persons (IDPs). The citizens of the host nation will never achieve social well-being if these three conditions are not met, and they will not be met without the support of a sustainable transportation network.[85]

The transportation infrastructure must consider the unique aspects of the culture that it serves in order to increase social values. There have been many failures with respect to infrastructure during stability operations. In 1966, the British built barracks with flushing toilets in Aden. Their failure to realize that the host nation Soldiers used rocks instead of paper resulted in the toilets being destroyed.[86] Similar unintended consequences can arise without proper consideration to culture when planning transportation. In Afghanistan, though roads were needed to help create a sustainable economy, as roads helped extend the influence of the central government, they might have worked against the stable governance sector due to the population's hostility toward the central government. Units conducting PSOs must understand culture to garner cooperation.

Comprehensive Approach

Achieving success in PSO, HA operations, or assisting developing countries to move further from the possibility of conflict is much more likely when employing a whole of government concept. Implemented over time, a whole of government approach lowers long term costs, reduces the risk of objectives being compromised, and increases legitimacy. An example of this can be found in the Special Inspector General's lessons learned from Iraq where numerous programs from 15 government agencies are listed.[87] Beyond this, however, is the need to also achieve unity of effort with all potential sources of contributions, such as the numerous non-governmental organizations, international organizations, academia, and the private sector from the host nation, the United States, and coalition partners. A common mistake when developing infrastructure like transportation is for the product or service to develop quicker than the institutions and regulations to sustain the system. This is less likely to occur when working in a whole of government, inter-agency, collaborative approach. There is tremendous synergy to be gained by including the private sector. With respect to transportation, the private sector can defer large capital costs and stand to make handsome profits by ensuring critical nodes are run efficiently. Successful examples include "rail privatization in Mozambique, port privatization in Argentina, the privatization of customs functions in Indonesia, and the establishment of operating contracts for cold cargo facilities in India and Chile."[88] Finally, the importance of working with and through the host nation cannot be overemphasized. Working cooperatively and in collaboration with the host nation serves to bolster the long term vision, synchronize transportation proj-ects, ensure maintenance of the system by the long term owner, and has the important secondary benefit of building the credibility of the host nation govern-ment.[89]

Conclusions and Recommendations
Domestic

Sustainable transportation is a critical interest of the United States. Now is the time for a comprehen-sive U.S. policy which lays out a long term vision and incorporates the key elements of sustainable transpor-tation to include transportation resilience, economic development, environmental health, and social values. With the poor condition of transportation infrastruc-ture in the United States presently, an opportunity is at hand to leverage political and popular will to cast a vision and lay new ground work for sustainability that balances all four of these essential components. The strategic vision for sustainable transportation will enable the movement of people, goods, and services in a multi-modal system and a manner that meets current and future needs. Implementing this vision requires a comprehensive whole of government approach.

Emphasis on transportation resilience domestically should focus upon redundant and reliable delivery systems and tear down the historic view of transportation policy and laws in separate modes. Rather than separating surface, air, maritime, and pipeline modes into separate transportation bills, a comprehensive approach will integrate laws, regulations, policies, and performance measures to ensure resilient transportation systems regardless of mode. This comprehensive approach will create opportunities for increased efficiency by considering overlap of common resilience needs such as security and defense systems, emergency repair and response, and safety. While gaining efficiencies in these areas, transportation resilience will naturally induce competition by promoting parallel delivery systems that are also consistent with the sustainable transportation component of economic development.

As a first principle of economic development related to sustainable transportation, domestic transportation must have a sustainable financing mechanism. The failure of the past several years is demonstrated by the perennial transfers from the General Fund to the Highway Trust Fund to prevent insolvency due to inadequate receipts versus expenses. A long term funding solution for public sector investments, which in turn attracts private sector development, must be found. User fees or taxes by modality provide equity for transportation system benefactors, but with sustainable transportation as a national strategic interest, a percentage of underwriting from general funds is justified if couched in a long term vision. Where critical gaps in resilience exist, economic incentives should be established that promote new transportation modes or protection of limited systems available for such things as hurricane evacuations or earthquake disaster response. Regional assessment of transportation maturity categories represented in Table 1 will allow benchmarking and prioritizing current needs and future investments by public agencies at the national, regional, and local levels in accordance with appropriate environmental health concerns and social values.

A comprehensive approach to sustainable transportation should elevate the linkage to health equity and access to economic opportunity, which demonstrates social value to both urban and rural areas. Sustainable transportation will enable health equity as it relates to the human environment, national goals for accessible healthcare, and access to jobs. A national transportation vision under President Eisenhower that focused on mobilization of the military in post-World War II could be moderized for the current century. A new sustainable transportation focus on evacuating regions pre-disaster, mobilizing emergency responders and health care providers post-disaster, protecting and expanding in-place transportation systems, and military mobilization in a post-hurricane Katrina/Sandy environment is at hand.

Deliberate policy that establishes a national long term transportation vision linked to other national policy goals and incorporates the four elements of sustainable transportation will enable prosperity and security now and in the future. While the domestic benefits of establishing a sustainable transportation vision are thus clearly established, the U.S. can apply these same principles during peace and stability operations around the globe.

Peace and Stability Operations (PSO)

As previously described, transportation was an extremely important component of the United States achieving world hegemony and the relatively recent rise of China. It stands to reason then that turning fragile countries into contributing members of the international community must place similar importance on the transportation sector. The key to success, however, will be tied to how well resilience, economic development, environmental health, and social values are prioritized and balanced as the transportation systems and infrastructure grow. In fragile states, or those where international actors are conducting PSO, it is also vital to link transportation efforts to the other stability sectors. Transportation improves security, justice, and economic stabilization by connecting the population to security forces, courts, and markets. Similarly, governance and participation is increased as the government extends its influence and citizens have access to the democratic process. In fact, these linkages are too numerous to list since transportation facilitates everything directly or indirectly. Success will only come if progress toward a safe and secure environment, rule of law, stable governance, sustainable economy, and social well-being occurs simultaneously with the development of transportation.

Long term vision is the bedrock for building success in fragile states and during PSO. Success is untenable without it. This is extremely poignant for military forces participating in PSO, because these units will almost certainly depart prior to achieving the long term vision. This fact should not undermine the importance of creating the vision that military, civilian, non-governmental, private, and international organizations must operate under to ensure accomplishment of synergistic goals. The best long term vision will even include the period of time when the stabilized nation is operating sans external assistance. Recent operations are rife with examples of failing to do this. For example, Afghanistan collected over $200 million in 2009 from transportation related activities, but instead of earmarking funds to maintain the infrastructure the revenue went into a general fund.[90] Long term vision must be established up front and projects have to be prioritized based on how well the vision is supported. If not, changes occurring will be moving along a vector that will not achieve the overarching goal.

Although transportation is critical to development progress, positive effects and success comes very slowly. The international community must therefore temper expectations. The United States generally plans 20 to 30 years out, but the appetite for PSOs that last that long does not exist. One but needs look at road construction in Afghanistan to see how long it takes to develop transportation. As of November 2013, 5,430 kms of roads were completed with 2,266 kms under construction.[91] There were almost no paved roads in 2001. Texas, a comparable land area, on the other hand, has 485,000 kms of roads, 382 public airports, and over 18,000 kms of railroads.[92] Afghanistan has less than 160 kms of railroad, is 2,000 kms from the nearest seaport, and relies on service and agriculture sectors that are obviously inhibited in connecting to customers and markets. Additionally, the international community is depending on the extractives industry to pick up the slack as aid declines, but these endeavors will face the same challenges.[93] Creating and improving transportation systems in fragile states must be linked to reasonable expectations of progress. Efforts must also be heavily concentrated on the capacity of the host nation. Progress will stall or cease to exist without strong policy, regulations, ways and means for collecting revenue, administrative competence, and decreased corruption. These are more important than the construction of a particular capability.

Somewhat related to the tempering of expectations is the balance that agencies and organizations must strike between short and long term projects. Short term projects can show immediate progress resulting in the government gaining support of the population. These projects might alleviate suffering, provide better access to water or markets, or start to invest in social capital at a relatively low cost such as when a school is built. Because the projects are low-cost, visibly demonstrate progress, and are easy to plan and execute, donors have a bias for executing them over the more complex long-term projects. The long-term projects are just as important as previously alluded to in the discussion on vision. Afghanistan, for example, will never achieve its status as the central Eurasian transportation hub (a modern silk road) if there is not an emphasis on airports, railroads, and access to ports. Likewise, a great portion of resources and effort must be placed on building the capacity to operate these facilities. This is much more difficult, because it includes policy, regulations, education, training, and systems that facilitate operations and revenue collection.

Another common mistake in PSO and in developing fragile states is not putting enough effort into understanding the environment prior to executing projects. Planners must have a full appreciation of the second and third order effects that will occur. The British in Aden inadvertently put locals out of business by building a road, because the preferred transporters shifted from locals with camels to truck drivers from the capital city once the road was complete. On the other hand, the projects supported by the local population garnered support to the point that they volunteered to secure the projects.[94] Many of the projects being executed in Afghanistan certainly do not have this visible level of support, which may explain why the ring road and Kabul to Herat road are still not complete. In fact, many places have fallen into disrepair following construction due to locals failing to secure the road from attacks. Understanding the second and third order effects of projects will enable donors to gain an appropriate amount of buy-in from the local population, thus, greatly improving the chances for long term success.

Planners must also have an acute appreciation for the culture of the society in which they are operating. Projects must have 'cultural buy-in' to be successful. The British campaign in Aden once again provides a good example of this. The indigenous Arabs destroyed flush toilets due to their cultural habit of using rocks rather than paper. A lack of appreciation for the culture resulted in these constructed facilities being useless while the locals returned to the use of deep trench latrines.[95] It is possible that a lack of cultural appreciation is the cause for slow progress in developing the road networks of Afghanistan. Theory and practice advocate for the need of roads and other transportation networks to connect the people to the government and provide the backbone for economic prosperity. Afghanistan, however, has a long history of not trusting their government. The numerous isolated tribes throughout the country did not have the same interest in securing transportation networks that connected them to a government they disliked. On the other hand, the World Bank and the Inter-American Development Bank were very successful in improving the road networks in Peru. This success can be attributed to the fact that,

Project managers held extensive consultations and preparatory workshops to: a) assess real transportation needs, b) understand poverty links as perceived by the community, c) confirm priority of works and the community's commitment to its maintenance, d) validate designs and include local solutions, e) mobilize local government support for road building and institution building, and finally, f) build up ownership with key stakeholders concerning strategies and proposed actions.[96]

It is safe to assume that these planners understood the culture of the host nation very well thanks to their detailed preparation.

As previously discussed, environmental health is an important, but often overlooked principle of sustainable transportation. Donor countries, international organizations, NGOs, forces conducting PSOs, and others must get better at synchronizing the development of transportation infrastructure with environmental health. A recent UNEP publication highlighted the risk to stability when illegal exploitation and poor management of natural resources exists. On the other hand, transportation can facilitate the efficient extraction, use, and export of natural resources which can pay large dividends to the host nation in the form of employment and revenue. UNEP's training in Afghanistan that includes "discussions...on the links between natural resource management and peacebuilding with a focus on how to integrate conflict sensitivity into project planning" is a definite step in the right direction.[97] The long term financial expenses, potential physical damage, and harm to the relationship with the host nation are all much too costly to ignore environmental health while developing transportation infrastructure.

The domestic risk-based strategies discussed above are also applicable to PSOs. Many PSOs focus on mitigating risk, but the other options of avoiding, transferring, and accepting risk should also be considered. In general, domestic planners will be much more likely to employ risk avoidance strategies when possible, even at a high cost. During PSOs, however, planners will be more likely to focus on mitigation or even risk acceptance. The bottom line is that all four of the risk strategies are applicable, both domestically and within fragile states, and the long term vision, expectations of stakeholders, cultural factors, and analysis of second and third order effects should determine which risk strategy is most appropriate.

Finally, those involved in planning and executing PSO and those working development in fragile states must continue to refine their assessment tools. Evaluating the worth of these and making recommendations for improvement is a paper in and of itself. Suffice it to say that we would be much further in the progress of Afghanistan if our assessments were adequate. Tools currently being used in the United States, such as the Interagency Conflict Assessment Framework (ICAF) or Measuring Progress in Conflict Environments (MPICE), should be updated with the requisite detail that assures satisfactory progress in the critically important area of transportation. These tools should incorporate metrics to assess the four principles of sustainable transportation described in this paper. The Federal Highway Administration's

(FHWA's) Infrastructure Voluntary Evaluation Sustainability Tool (INVEST) is an excellent resource to begin creating an assessment tool containing enough detail to adequately assess resilience, economic development, environmental health, and social values with respect to transportation development during PSOs. This is another area where domestic ways and means can inform PSOs executed overseas.

Endnotes

1. Richard F. Weingroff, "The Battle of Its Life," *Public Roads,* May/June 2006, Vol. 69, No. 6, *http://www.fhwa.dot.gov/publications/publicroads/06may/05.cfm* (accessed December 19, 2013).

2. UN Document, *Report of the World Commission on Environment and Development: Our Common Future,* Transmitted to the General Assembly as an Annex to document A/42/427 - Development and International Cooperation: Environment, (United Nations, 1987), 15.

3. Weingroff, "The Battle of Its Life."

4. Encyclopedia Britannica, *http://www.britannica.com/EBchecked/topic/508316/Roman-road-system* (accessed December 20, 2013).

5. Jean-Paul Rodrigue, "The Silk Road and Arab Sea Routes," *The Geography of Transport Systems,* Hofstra University, New York, 1998, *http://people.hofstra.edu/geotrans/eng/ch2en/conc2en/silkroad.html* (accessed February 11, 2014).

6. U.S.–China Economic Security and Review Commission, *2012 Report to Congress by the U.S.-China Economic Security and Review Commission* (Washington, D.C: U.S. Government Printing Office, November 2012), 1.

7. Temuri Yakobashvili, "A Chinese Marshall Plan for Central Asia?" *Central Asia-Caucasus Institute: Analytical Articles* (October 16, 2013).

8. *Ibid.*

9. Sun Tzu, translated by Lionel Giles, *The Art of War* (London: Department of Oriental Books and Manuscripts British Museum, 1910), 46.

10. U.S.–China Economic Security and Review Commission, *2012 Report to Congress*, 11.

11. Andrew Feickert, *The Unified Command Plan and Combatant Commands: Background and Issues for Congress* (Washington, DC: Library of Congress, Congressional Research Service, January 3, 2013), 24.

12. United States Department of Transportation, *Transportation Walk Exhibit* (1200 New Jersey Avenue Southeast, Washington, DC, viewed December 15, 2013).

13. *Ibid.*

14. The Miller Center-University of Virginia, *Are We There Yet? Selling America on Transportation: David R. Goode National Transportation Policy Conference Final Report,* (Charlottesville, VA: The Miller Center, November 2011), 9.

15. Feickert, *The Unified Command Plan and Combatant Commands*, 25.

16. UN Document, *Report of the World Commission on Environment and Development*, 15.

17. U.S. Department of Transportation, *INVEST User Guide,* (Washington, D.C: Federal Highway Administration, 2012), 1.

18. *Ibid.*

19. *Ibid.*

20. U.S. Institute of Peace and U.S. Army Peacekeeping and Stability Operations Institute, *Guiding Principles for Stabilization and Reconstruction,* (Washington, DC: U.S. Institute of Peace Press, 2009), 4-26.

21. *Ibid.*, 5-30.

22. *Ibid.*, 4-26.

23. Michael J. Savonis, Virginia R. Burkett, and Joanne R. Potter, *Impacts of Climate Variability and Change on Transportation Systems and Infrastructure, Gulf Coast Study: Synthesis and Assessment Product 4.7, Report by the U.S. Climate Change Science Program and the Subcommiittee on Global Change Research* (Washington, D.C: Department of Transportation), 7.

24. American Association of State Highway and Transportation Officials, *AASHTO Transportation Asset Management Guide, A Focus On Implementation, Executive Summary* (Washington, D.C.: AASHTO and U.S. Department of Transportation, June 2013), 6.

25. *Ibid.*, 2.

26. Savonis, Burkett, and Potter, *Impacts of Climate Variability*, 206.

27. Bahar Barami, "Infrastructure Resiliency: A Risk-Based Framework," White Paper, Center for Transportation and Logistics Security, The John A. Volpe National Transportation Systems Center, U.S. Department of Transportation, Cambridge, MA, June 2013, 1.

28. Marc Mandler, "Volpe Speaker Series Examines Ways to Enhance Transportation System Resilience," Event Announcement, The John A. Volpe National Transportation Systems Center, U.S. Department of Transportation, Cambridge, MA, November 7, 2013.

29. Barami, "Infrastructure Resiliency," 2.

30. U.S. Department of Homeland Security, *2010 Transportation Systems Sector-Specific Plan, An Annex to the National Infrastructure Protection Plan* (Washington, D.C: Department of Homeland Security, 2010), 3.

31. Marc Mandler, "Volpe Speaker Series Examines Ways to Enhance Transportation System Resiliency", *DOT Net,* November 7, 2013 *http://dotnet.dot.gov/news/stories/2013/11/2013-11-07-Volpe-Speaker-Series.html* (accessed November 12, 2013).

32. Barami, "Infrastructure Resiliency," 3.

33. *Ibid.*

34. *Ibid.*, 3, 8.

35. *Ibid.*, 3.

36. *Ibid.*, 10, 11.

37. Office of Asset Management, Federal Highway Administration, *Risk-Based Asset Management: Examining Risk-Based Approaches to Transportation Asset Management, Report 2* (Washington, D.C.: U.S. Department of Transportation, 2012), 45.

38. Transportation Research Board, *Adapting Transportation to the Impacts of Climate Change, State of the Practice 2011, Transportation Research Circular E-C152* (Washington, D.C.: Transportation Research Board of the National Academies, 2011), 6.

39. Barami, "Infrastructure Resiliency," 5.

40. Addis Ababa, "Infrastructure Development as Catalyst for Economic Growth in Africa," Thematic Paper jointly prepare by African Union Commission and The New Partnership for Africa's Development, 17th Africa Partnership Forum, November 16, 2011, 1.

41. USIP and PKSOI, *Guiding Principles*, 9-132, 136, 139.

42. U.S. Agency for International Development, *A Guide to Economic Growth in Post-Conflict Countries* (Washington, D.C: Office of Economic Growth, Bureau for Economic Growth, Agriculture, and Trade, USAID, January 2009), 1.

43. *Ibid.*, 7.

44. Barami, "Infrastructure Resiliency," 5.

45. Department of Transportation, *INVEST User Guide*, 8.

46. United Nations Environment Programme and Development Alternatives, *South Asia Environment Outlook*, (Nairobi, Kenya, 2009), 30.

47. Michael Thrasher, "Beijing Air Pollution at Dangerously High Levels," *Huffington Post*, January 16, 2014

48. William Laurance, "As Roads Spread in Rainforest, the Environmental Toll Grows," *Environment360*, January 19, 2012.

49. Denis Rewerts, *Final Environmental Impact Statement, Tier 1 FAA Approval and Land Acquisition by the State of Illinois for Proposed South Suburban Airport*, (Des Plaines, IL: Federal Aviation Administration, 2003), Chapter 5.

50. World Bank Publication, *Development in Practice: Sustainable Transport, Priorities for Policy Reform*, (Washington, D.C.: The International Bank for Reconstruction Development-The World Bank, 1996), 50

51. Department of Transportation, *INVEST User Guide*, 11.

52. Barami, "Infrastructure Resiliency," 5.

53. Department of Transportation, *INVEST User Guide*, 12.

54. USIP and PKSOI, *Guiding Principles*, 5-31.

55. Frank Hoffman and Michael C. Davies, "Joint Force 2020 and the Human Domain: Time for a New Conceptual Framework", *Small Wars Journal*, June 10, 2013.

56. Department of Transportation, *INVEST User Guide*, 12.

57. USIP and PKSOI, *Guiding Principles*, 3-12, 5-30.

58. Agency for International Development, *A Guide to Economic Growth*, 7.

59. Rudolf Zauner, "Humanitarian Assistance and the Difficult Transition to Sustainable Development," Peace Keeping and Stability Operations Institute Electives Course PS2219-Concepts and Principles, member perspectives post May 31, 2013.

60. Department of Transportation, *INVEST User Guide,*14.

61. The Miller Center, *Are We There Yet?*, 13.

62. Amanda Bayhi, "Foxx: Highway Trust Fund on Track to Bounce Checks Before FY 2015", *Better Roads,* February 21, 2014.

63. American Society of Civil Engineers, *2013 Report Card for America's Infrastructure* Baltimore, MD: 2013, *http://www.infrastructurereportcard.org/a/#p/overview/executive-summary* (accessed December 28, 2013).

64. The Miller Center-University of Virginia, *A Blueprint for Presidential Leadership: David R. Goode National Transportation Policy Conference Final Report,* (Charlottesville, VA: The Miller Center, November 2013), 20.

65. USIP and PKSOI, *Guiding Principles*, 3-23, 6-56, 7-80, 9-150, 9-151, and 10-181; U.S. Joint Chiefs of Staff, *Stability Operations,* Joint Publication 3-07 (Washington DC: U.S. Joint Chiefs of Staff, September 29, 2011), xxii, I-22, III-9, and III-20; North Atlantic Treaty Organization, *Peace Support Operations,* Allied Joint Publication 3.4.1 (Military Agency for Standarisation, July 2001), 6-10.

66. Russell W. Glenn, *Core Counterinsurgency Asset: Lessons from Iraq and Afghanistan for United States Army Corps of Engineers Leaders,* (Washington, DC: U.S. Army Corps of Engineers, May 31, 2012), 8 – 14, 18, 20.

67. The World Bank, *World Development Report 2014: Risk and Opportunity – Managing Risk for Development,* (Washington, DC: International Bank for Reconstruction and Development, 2013), 38; African Union Commission, *Infrastructure Development as Catalyst for Economic Growth in Africa,* (Addis Ababa, Ethiopia: 17th Africa Partnership Forum, November 16, 2011), 3; U.S. Joint Forces Command, *Handbook for Military Support to Essential Services and*

Critical Infrastructure, Unified Action Handbook Series Book Two (Suffolk, VA: Joint Concept Development and Experimentation, February 2, 2010), II-4; Glenn, *Core Counterinsurgency Asset*, 31; Schaun J. Wheeler and Daniel I. Stolkowski, *Administrative Revision: Afghanistan: The Effectiveness of Development as a Component of Counterinsurgency Strategy*, (Charlottesville, VA: National Ground Intelligence Center, November 7, 2011), 1; S. Frederick Starr and Andrew C. Kuchins, *The Key to Success in Afghanistan: A Modern Silk Road Strategy*, (Washington, DC: Central Asia-Caucasus Institute and Silk Road Studies Program, May, 2010), 14, 17 – 19, 22, 32.

68. Rosemary DiCarlo, "U.S. Mission to the United Nations: Remarks at a Security Council Debate on Afghanistan," New York, NY, December 17, 2013.

69. S. Frederick Starr, *Finish the Job: Jump-Start Afghanistan's Economy*, (Washington, DC: Central Asia-Caucasus Institute and Silk Road Studies Program, November, 2012), 29 – 31; Stuart W. Bowen, Jr., "Learning From Iraq," A Final Report From the Special Inspector General for Iraq Reconstruction, March, 2013, 87 – 88.

70. The World Bank, *World Development Report 2014*, 85, 238; John F. Sopko, *Quarterly Report to the United States Congress*, (Arlington, VA: Special Inspector General for Afghanistan Reconstruction, July 30, 2013), 165; Keith Crane et al., *Guidebook for Supporting Economic Development in Stability Operations*, (Arlington, VA: RAND Corporation, 2009), 94.

71. USIP and PKSOI, *Guiding Principles*, 6-56.

72. Hillary Rodham Clinton, *Leading Through Civilian Power: The First Quadrennial Diplomacy and Development Review* (Washington, DC: 2010), 128.

73. Joint Forces Command, *Handbook for Military Support*, II-17.

74. Crane et al., *Guidebook for Supporting Economic Development*, 9, 37, 41.

75. Wheeler and Stolkowski, *Administrative Revision: Afghanistan*, 7.

76. USIP and PKSOI, *Guiding Principles,* 2-8.

77. Mary C. Ott, *A Guide to Economic Growth in Post-Conflict Countries* (Washington, DC: Office of Economic Growth, Bureau for Economic Growth, Agriculture and Trade, U.S. Agency for International Development, January, 2009), 1.

78. *Ibid.,* 40, 84.

79. Embassy of the United States of America, *Better Infrastructure Brings Economic Growth,* (Washington, DC: Bureau of International Information Programs, U.S. Department of State, June, 2012), 1; Leif Rosenberger, *How Smart Economic Strategy Could Strengthen the Afghan Counterinsurgency,* (Carlisle Barracks, PA: Strategic Studies Institute, February 10, 2011), 1-2; The World Bank, *World Development Report 2014,* 125; The World Bank, *Afghanistan in Transition: Looking Beyond 2014, Volume 2: Main Report,* (Washington DC: The World Bank, May, 2012), 87; Crane et al., *Guidebook for Supporting Economic Development,* 57, 71, 110.

80. Francis Caas, Yoko Hagiwara and David Jensen, "Environmental Reconstruction of Conflict and Disaster Areas," http:// www.frida.no/publications/et/ep3/page/2612.aspx (accessed March 5, 2014).

81. Clay Risen, "The Environmental Consequences of War: Why militaries almost never clean up the messes they leave behind," *http://www.washingtonmonthly.com/features/2010/1001.risen. html* (accessed March 5, 2014).

82. United Nations Environment Programme, "In Defence of the Environment, Putting Poverty to the Sword," *http://www.unep. org/Documents.Multilingual/Default.asp?ArticleID=3810&Document ID=288* (accessed March 5, 2014).

83. Dina Fine Maron, The New York Times, "Pentagon Weighs Cleanups as It Plans Iraq Exit," *http://www.nytimes. com/gwire/2010/01/13/13greenwire-pentagon-weighs-cleanups-as-it-plans-iraq-exit-21915.html?pagewanted=all* (accessed March 5, 2014).

84. The Sphere Project, "Humanitarian Charter and Minimum Standards in Humanitarian Response," *http://www.sphere-handbook.org/* (accessed March 6, 2014).

85. USIP and PKSOI, *Guiding Principles*, 10-162.

86. Glenn, *Core Counterinsurgency Asset*, 16.

87. Anne Friederike Röder, ed. *Whole of Government Approaches to Fragile States*, (Paris, France: Organisation for Economic Co-operation and Development, 2006), 7; Bowen, Jr., "Learning From Iraq," 147 – 148.

88. Ott, *A Guide to Economic Growth*, 47.

89. Crane et al., *Guidebook for Supporting Economic Development*, 33 – 34.

90. The World Bank, *Afghanistan in Transition*, 97.

91. Department of Defense, *Report on Progress Toward Security and Stability in Afghanistan* (Washington, D.C: Report to Congress, November 2013), 105.

92. Bureau of Transportation Statistics, United States Department of Transportation, *http://www.rita.dot.gov/bts/sites/rita.dot.gov.bts/files/publications/state_transportation_statistics/texas/html/fast_facts.html* (accessed April 10, 2014).

93. Sopko, *Quarterly Report to the United States Congress*, 164.

94. Glenn, *Core Counterinsurgency Asset*, 16-17.

95. *Ibid.*, 16.

96. Joint Forces Command, *Handbook for Military Support*, III-12 – III-13.

97. United Nations Environment Programme, *Special Issue Newsletter: Natural Resources and Peacebuilding* (New York: Peacebuilding Support Office, April 2014), 4, 10.